THE FOLLOWERS OF JESUS

THE FOLLOWERS
OF
JESUS

Published by
Christian Focus Publications Ltd.

© Christian Focus Publications 1992
ISBN 1871676 894

Illustrated by Morna Whyte
Written by Carine Mackenzie
Layout and Design by Seoris N. McGillivray

•C•F•P•

CONTENTS

THE FOLLOWERS OF JESUS

TWELVE SPECIAL MEN

Those who love the Lord Jesus will want to be taught by him and to follow him. They will imitate his example. They will want to do what pleases him.

Jesus asked twelve men to be his special followers. They were very close to him, spending a lot of time with him.

He asked them to preach the good news about his salvation to others. He gave them power to heal people who were sick and to drive away evil spirits.

Their names were Simon Peter, James, John, Andrew, Philip, Nathaniel, Matthew, Thomas, another James, Thaddaeus, another Simon, and Judas Iscariot.

What
did they do ?

'He appointed twelve — calling them apostles
— that they might be with him and that he
might send them out to preach and to have
authority to drive out demons.'

(Mark 3. 14-15)

Peter

Simon and his brother Andrew were fishermen from Bethsaida on the Sea of Galilee. One day Andrew heard John the Baptist describe Jesus as the lamb of God who takes away the sin of the world. Andrew along with a friend spent the rest of the day with Jesus. They realised that he was the Christ, the Saviour sinners. Andrew quickly told Simon the go news and took his brother to meet Jesus himself.

Jesus gave Simon a new name. He called h PETER, which means 'a stone'. Jesus visit Peter at home after worshipping at the synag gue. Peter's mother-in-law was very sick. I ter told Jesus, who immediately healed he

Sometimes Jesus used Peter's boat as I platform when he taught the people on t shores of the Sea of Galilee. On one occasi Jesus displayed his power to Peter and t other people with him by causing them catch a huge amount of fish. Peter was ve impressed by Jesus' power. He fell down his knees and worshipped him.

'Don't be afraid,' Jesus said to them. 'Fro now on you will work for me. Follow me an will make you "fishers of men".'

Peter's new work was to tell people the go news about Jesus.

Peter followed Jesus closely as he moved through the country preaching and teaching and healing sick people and doing good. He remained loyal to Jesus even when some other followers turned away from Jesus. Jesus was upset by these people going away. He asked his disciples if they would also go away. Peter answered for them by insisting that they were convinced that Jesus was the only one who could give them eternal life.

Yet he proudly thought that he would always be brave and faithful to Jesus. Sadly this was not so. When Jesus was being falsely accused by the authorities just before his cruel death on the cross, Peter denied on three occasions that he even knew Jesus. As he denied the third time, Jesus turned and looked at Peter. What a disappointment to Jesus! How did Peter felt! But Jesus does not reject those who love him and follow him even when they sin.

After Jesus died on the cross he rose again from the dead by the power of God. Many people saw him and spoke with him, including Peter. At a meal early one morning by the sea of Galilee, Jesus asked Peter three times, 'Do you love me?' 'You know that I love you,' replied Peter.

Later, Jesus gave Peter the task of spreading the good news of salvation to the whole world. On the Day of Pentecost and during the following weeks, he preached boldly to thousands of people urging them to repent and turn from their sins and be baptized in the name of Jesus Christ.

The religious leaders and officials did not like what Peter was preaching. They had him thrown into prison. But God was with him. An angel of the Lord opened the prison door at night and led Peter to freedom — back to preaching about Jesus.

Peter spent the rest of his life travelling to different countries preaching the gospel to many people and teaching them how to live a life pleasing to Jesus. He wrote two letters to Christians which are now part of the Bible.

James and John

James and John were brothers, both working as fishermen on the Sea of Galilee. They were in partnership with Peter and his brother, Andrew. All of them saw Jesus' immense power over the fish of the sea. When Jesus caused Peter's net to fill with a huge catch of fishes, James and John had to hurry to help him pull the catch to the shore.

Jesus saw them one day mending their fishing nets with their father Zebedee. Jesus asked them to follow him and they immediately left their nets and their fishing business to become followers and helpers of the Lord Jesus.

Their lives were completely changed. Their days were no longer filled with fishing trips, mending nets or selling fish. They accompanied Jesus around the country, hearing him teaching crowds of people and watching him heal the sick.

Along with Peter they were chosen to witness a wonderful event when Jesus took the three men up a high mountain. Miraculously Jesus' appearance changed — his face shone

like the sun and even his clothes became shining white. Moses and Elijah appeared talking to Jesus. God spoke from heaven, 'This is my Son, whom I love: with him I am well pleased. Listen to him.'

The men fell down on the ground terrified but Jesus reassured them, telling them not to be afraid.

Jesus was especially close to Peter, James and John. While he was praying in the Garden of Gethsemane on the night before his death, he asked them to come apart from the others and watch with him. As Jesus was praying, they were so tired they fell asleep.

John was specially loved by Jesus. When Jesus was hanging on the cross he spoke to John and asked him to look after his mother, Mary. Even in his extreme suffering Jesus thought of others. He told Mary that John would be like a son to her. From then on John took Mary to live in his own house.

After Jesus' death the disciples were sad and disappointed. Three days later Jesus rose from the dead. Mary Magdalene came to tell that the grave was empty. Peter and John ran to find out for themselves. John reached there first. They were both amazed to find the grave clothes neatly folded and no sign of the body of Jesus.

Later that day Jesus appeared to the disciples as they met secretly in a house. They were overjoyed.

James and John and others began to preach and teach about Jesus and tell others about the salvation offered to those who trust in Jesus the Lord. They faced many dangers and a lot of opposition. King Herod was against those who preached the gospel. He arrested many who belonged to the church including James. He ordered James to be killed by a sword — martyred for his faith.

John lived until old age. He was inspired by the Holy Spirit to write one of the Gospels telling about Jesus Christ, the Son of God and encouraging people to believe in him. John also wrote three important letters to the Christian church, and the book of Revelation which encourages Christians to stand firmly with Christ's help against Satan.

Philip, Nathaniel, Matthew and Thomas

Philip heard the Lord Jesus say to him, 'Follow me.' He willingly did so. He found his friend Nathaniel and told him that the Messiah spoken about in the Old Testament was actually here in person — 'Jesus of Nazareth'.

'Nazareth! Can anything good come from that wicked place?' asked Nathaniel in amazement.

'Come and see for yourself,' replied Philip.

When Jesus saw Nathaniel coming he announced, 'Here is a true man. There is nothing false in him.'

'How do you know me?' exclaimed Nathaniel.

'I saw you even before Philip called you, when you were under the fig tree,' replied Jesus.

Nathaniel was struck by Jesus' knowledge of him. 'You are the Son of God,' he confessed.

All the disciples spent time with Jesus. They heard his wise teaching; they saw him do marvellous things.

Matthew was a tax collector. One day Jesus walked past his booth while Matthew was working. 'Follow me,' said Jesus. Matthew immediately left his work to answer Jesus' call and become one of his disciples.

That evening Jesus had dinner at Matthew's house. Many other tax collectors and sinners were also guests at the meal. The Jewish leaders were annoyed to see Jesus mixing with such people. Jesus told them, 'Healthy people do not need a doctor; sick people do. Sinners need me, the Saviour.'

Another of Jesus' disciples was called Thomas. He was not in the company on the Lord's Day evening when Jesus, risen from the dead, appeared to the gathered disciples. When the others told him about it, he refused to believe them. 'I won't believe,' he said, 'unless I can put my fingers into the prints of the nails in his hands and put my hand into the wound made by the spear in his side.' Poor doubting Thomas!

On the next Lord's Day Thomas was with the other disciples when the Lord Jesus appeared to them again. Jesus knew of Thomas' doubts.

'Put your fingers here in my hands,' he said to him. 'Put your hand in my side. Stop doubting. Just believe.'

Thomas did believe. 'My Lord and my God,' he exclaimed.

THE FOLLOWERS OF JESUS
ALL KINDS OF PEOPLE

Many people met Jesus and heard him preach and teach. Many lives were changed after they met Jesus. Some were healed of diseases: some repented of their sin: some had loved ones raised from the dead.

Jesus called himself the Good Shepherd.

Those who love him are called his sheep. The Good Shepherd knows his sheep and cares for them. The sheep follow the Good Shepherd.

All kinds of people followed the Lord Jesus — women, who were not always highly thought of: important rulers: ordinary people and even children.

Who were they ?

'My sheep listen to my voice; I know them,
and they follow me.'

(John 10.27)

Two Ladies

Jesus was travelling back from Galilee to Judea. He had to go through the region of Samaria. He was so tired and thirsty. At midday he sat down on a well near Sychar to have a rest, while his disciples went into the town to buy food.

A woman from Sychar came to the well to draw water. Although she was an immoral woman Jesus did not ignore her. 'Will you give me a drink?' he asked. The woman replied rather rudely, referring to the old quarrel between the Jewish people like Jesus and the Samaritans like herself.

Jesus patiently and kindly told her about himself. If she followed him he would satisfy her longing heart even more than the water would satisfy her thirst. She should come to Jesus and follow him in spite of her sinful life.

The Lord Jesus knew all about her sins but he would forgive her. He told her plainly that he was Jesus Christ, the Son of God. She believed in him and left her waterpot at the well to go to tell other people about the Lord Jesus. She loved and trusted him and became one of his followers.

Another lady who loved and followed Jesus was Mary Magdalene. Her life had been full of trouble and unhappiness, but Jesus changed her life completely. She, and other women who had been helped or cured by Jesus, followed him and the disciples from town to town listening to him preaching the good news of the kingdom of God. She used some of her own money to help support them in this work.

When Jesus was cruelly killed on the cross, Mary Magdalene was close by watching. How sad she must have felt. She was surprised to see two important Jewish officials taking his body from the cross.

She and a friend followed them and saw them put his body in a rich man's tomb. They watched as a big stone was rolled over the entrance. Soldiers were placed on guard.

Three days later, very early in the morning, Mary Magdalene and a friend made their way again to the tomb hoping to anoint Jesus' body with spices. What a surprise! The stone had been rolled back and a bright shining angel sat on it. 'Don't be afraid,' he said. 'You are looking for Jesus. He is not here. He has risen.'

Scared and bewildered Mary Magdalene turned away from the tomb. She walked in the garden weeping. 'Why are you crying?' she heard a voice say.

'Sir, if you have taken away the body of my Lord Jesus, tell me where you have laid him,' she replied to the man she thought was the gardener.

'Mary,' she heard.

Immediately she recognised the voice of Jesus. He had indeed risen from the dead. What joy she felt. She shared her wonderful news with the disciples: 'I have seen the Lord.'

Two Rulers

Nicodemus was well educated and held an important position on the council of rulers. He heard about the wonderful things Jesus was doing. One dark night he came to see Jesus. He was afraid to be seen speaking to him so he came secretly.

'No one can belong to the kingdom of God,' Jesus told him, 'unless he is born again.'

Nicodemus was puzzled by this. 'How could a grown-up man be born for a second time?' he wondered.

How lovingly they would have taken Jesus' body from the cross and carried him to the tomb. They anointed the body with myrrh and aloes and wrapped it in strips of linen.

Both Joseph and Nicodemus were secret followers of Jesus at one time but they openly admitted by their words and actions that they did love the Lord Jesus. They did so bravely at a time when Jesus' other disciples had run away and were in hiding.

Jesus explained to him that being born again means to have a new life, to start afresh by trusting in the Lord Jesus.

Jesus told many wonderful things to Nicodemus that night. He told him of God's great love for all the people in the world — so great that he sent his own dear Son to the world to die, so that those who believe in him would not perish but have everlasting life.

After that night Nicodemus followed Jesus more openly. At one council meeting some of the members were raging at the guards for not arresting Jesus. The guards had been impressed by Jesus' words. The council members were rude and indignant. Nicodemus spoke up courageously, 'Is it part of our law to condemn a man before we hear him? Surely not!'

Joseph from Arimathea was another secret follower of Jesus at first. He too was an important ruler in Jerusalem. After the death of Jesus, he bravely went to Pilate to ask for Jesus' body so that he could bury it respectfully in his own new tomb — a cave in the hillside. Nicodemus helped him.

The Family at Bethany

Mary and Martha and their brother Lazarus were a happy family, who lived in the town of Bethany. They were friends of Jesus. Sometimes he came to their house for a meal.

One supper time Martha was busy preparing a special meal for Jesus. Her sister Mary was sitting down beside Jesus listening to his wise words. Martha was upset about this. 'Ask my sister to help me,' complained Martha.

'Don't be so bothered about serving the food, Martha,' said Jesus. 'Mary is doing the best thing.'

Some time later Martha and Mary were very worried. Lazarus was sick. 'Let's send for Jesus,' they suggested. 'He will be able to help us.'

Jesus received their message but he did not immediately rush to Bethany. Lazarus died. By the time Jesus reached Bethany, Lazarus had been dead and buried for four days. As soon as Martha heard that Jesus was coming, she ran out of the house to meet him. Mary stayed at home.

'If only you had been here, Lazarus would not have died,' cried Martha. 'Your brother will rise again,' Jesus assured her.

Martha returned to the house to tell Mary that Jesus had come. Mary went to greet him with the same sad message.

They took Jesus to the place where Lazarus was buried. Jesus wept there. 'Take the stone away,' Jesus ordered to everyone's amazement. The order was carried out. Jesus prayed to God the Father, then shouted loudly, 'Lazarus, come out.' Lazarus walked out of the grave still wearing the linen graveclothes. Mary and Martha were overjoyed.

Many people who saw this miracle for themselves believed in Jesus, and became his followers too.

Some time later Jesus was again at supper in Bethany. Martha was helping to serve. Mary came into the room with a very expensive jar of ointment. She poured all of it over Jesus' feet and wiped his feet with her hair. She did this to show Jesus how much she loved him.

Judas Iscariot, who later betrayed Jesus, complained at this extravagance but Jesus was pleased with what she had done.

Children

Jesus had time for children too. Once, little children were brought to Jesus. Their parents wanted Jesus to pray for them. The disciples were annoyed about this and told them to go away.

'Let the little children come to me,' said Jesus. 'Do not keep them away. The kingdom of heaven belongs to little ones like them.'

Jesus took them up in his arms, put his hands on them and blessed them.

Other youngsters heard him preaching and teaching. One was even used as an example when Jesus was teaching his disciples a lesson. They had been arguing about who would be the greatest. Jesus called a little child over to stand beside him.

'The person who is humble like this little child,' said Jesus, 'will be the greatest in the kingdom of heaven.'

Several sick children were healed and restored by Jesus.

One royal official from Capernaum had a little boy who was very sick — very close to death.

'Please come to see my son before he dies,' the father begged Jesus.

'Your son will live,' Jesus replied. 'Go back home.'

The man took Jesus at his word and went off home. Before he reached the house, his servants came running out to meet him.

'Your son is better,' they exclaimed. He had recovered at the exact time that Jesus had spoken to the father. The whole household believed in Jesus and became his followers.

A little girl aged twelve was also healed by Jesus.

Her father, Jairus, was an important man in the church (called synagogue). His daughter became very ill. Jairus went to find Jesus to tell him the problem. Jesus took time on the way to heal a sick lady. By the time they reached Jairus' house, the girl had died.

'Don't be afraid,' Jesus comforted Jairus. 'Only believe.'

Jesus went into the house with the grieving family. Lovingly he said, 'Little girl, get up.' She was restored to life. Immediately the little girl got out of bed. 'Bring her something to eat,' ordered Jesus. Jesus had a care for all her needs.

Many others were healed in their bodies and minds.

THE FOLLOWERS OF JESUS

SENT ALL AROUND THE WORLD

Three days after Jesus had died, he rose again to life. The disciples and many other people saw him. He gave an important message to his disciples before he left the world to ascend into heaven.

He wanted the good news of salvation to be spread all round the world. God, the Holy Spirit, would give Jesus' followers the power to do this.

Where did they go ?

'Go and make disciples of all nations baptising them in the name of the Father and of the Son and of the Holy Spirit, and teaching them to obey everything I have commanded you. And surely I am with you always, to the very end of the age.'

(Matthew 28.19-20)

The Day of Pentecost

Jesus left the world from the Mount of Olives to return to heaven. He told the disciples to wait for the Holy Spirit to be sent to help them witness for him.

His followers went back to Jerusalem. His mother Mary and his brothers met with the disciples in an upstairs room. They spent all the time praying together.

People from many nations were visiting Jerusalem for the feast of Pentecost. The Feast of Pentecost (which means fifty) was on the fiftieth day after the Passover. It marked the beginning of the harvest thanksgiving.

The disciples were together in one house. Suddenly the noise of a strong wind filled the house. Separate tongues of fire rested on each one. The Holy Spirit filled them with his power. This had the amazing result that they could speak God's word to the crowds in Jerusalem and each man heard what they were saying in his own language.

The crowds were amazed. But some made fun of them. 'They have had too much to drink,' they jeered.

Peter stood up and addressed the crowd. 'We have not drunk any wine,' he said. 'It is only nine o'clock in the morning.'

He continued preaching the good news of Jesus to them, telling them of his death and resurrection, and urging them to repent, to accept Jesus' forgiveness of sins and to be baptised.

On that one day about three thousand people believed in Jesus Christ and became his followers.

Dorcas and Cornelius

In the seaside town of Joppa lived a good lady called Dorcas. She loved the Lord. She was a follower of Jesus. She served the Lord in practical ways. She made clothes for poor families; she helped widows and children as much as she could.

Dorcas became ill and died. Her body was placed in an upstairs room.

Her friends heard that Peter was in the near-by town of Lydda. They sent two men there immediately. They begged Peter to come to Joppa at once.

Peter arrived soon at Dorcas' house. When he went into the room, he found many women there weeping. 'Look at this garment that Dorcas made for me,' one said to Peter.

Peter asked them all to leave the room. Then he got down on his knees and prayed. He turned to Dorcas and said, 'Get up!' Immediately she opened her eyes. As soon as she saw Peter in her room, she sat up. He took her hand and helped her to her feet. He called to the friends to come back. Dorcas was well again. Peter had performed this miracle by the power of God. News travelled all round Joppa and many other people believed in the Lord and became followers of Jesus.

North of Joppa in the town of Caesarea lived a Roman soldier called Cornelius. He was a religious man who prayed regularly to God and who was kind to the poor. One afternoon he had a vision. He clearly saw an angel who said to him, 'Send to Joppa for Peter to come to your house.'

Cornelius sent two servants and a soldier to find Peter. When they arrived Peter was on the roof-top thinking about a vision he had received from the Lord, preparing him for this event. God, the Holy Spirit, instructed Peter to go with these men.

Cornelius was waiting for them. A large company of his friends had gathered to hear God's message to them through Peter.

Peter preached to the gathering, telling them that Jesus has followers from every nation. He told them about Jesus' miracles, his death and wonderful resurrection.

'Everyone who believes in him receives forgiveness of sin,' proclaimed Peter.

Cornelius and his friends believed the message and were filled with the Holy Spirit. They became followers of the Lord Jesus and were baptised.

Stephen

Stephen was a devout follower of the Lord
Jesus. He was chosen to look after the daily
distribution of food to the poor. He did many
miracles through God's power. By the help of
the Holy Spirit, he spoke very wisely. Some of
the Jewish leaders argued with Stephen but
his wise words always defeated them.

They wickedly persuaded men to accuse
Stephen falsely with blasphemy against God.
Stephen was seized and brought before the
high court of the Jews. Several people told lies

about Stephen and his message. 'He speaks against this place and against the law. He wants to change our customs and laws,' they said.

'Are these charges true?' asked the high priest. Stephen stood up to reply, his face shining like an angel. Certainly the Lord was with him, helping to find the right words. Stephen reminded the assembled priests of what God had done for the Jewish nation in the past and how they had rebelled against him. He accused them boldly of murdering the Lord Jesus. The priests were furious at what Stephen had said.

Stephen, full of the Holy Spirit, looked up to heaven and had a glimpse of the Lord Jesus.

'Look!' he said, 'I see heaven open and Jesus standing at the right hand of God.'

The Jewish priests became absolutely incensed with rage. Yelling at the top of their voices they rushed at Stephen and dragged him out of the temple, right out of the city.

They took off their cloaks and laid them on the ground at the feet of a young man called Saul.

They picked up big stones and hurled them at Stephen. 'Lord Jesus, receive my spirit,' he prayed. Just before he died, he prayed for the people who were killing him: 'Lord, do not hold this sin against them,' he pled.

Stephen showed real Christian love to his enemies.

Philip and the Ethiopian

Philip, a deacon from Jerusalem, preached about Christ in Samaria. People flocked to hear him and to see the miracles that he did by the power of God. Many people were healed. There was great joy all over the town.

Then, an angel spoke to Philip guiding him to make a journey. 'Go south,' he was told, 'to the desert road that goes from Jerusalem to Gaza.'

Philip started out on his journey and soon met an Ethiopian man. He had an important position in charge of the treasury of Candace, queen of Ethiopia. He was returning home from Jerusalem where he had been worshipping in the temple.

He was reading a scroll of the book of Isaiah in his chariot. Philip was guided by God, the Holy Spirit, to approach the chariot. He heard the man reading aloud from Isaiah.

'Do you understand what you are reading?' asked Philip.

'How can I?' he replied, 'unless someone explains it to me. Come up here and sit with me.'

The part that he was reading referred to a man who was like a lamb led to the slaughter and a sheep silent before its shearer.

'Who does Isaiah mean by that?' the Ethiopian asked. 'Is he speaking about himself or someone else?'

So Philip explained that Isaiah was speaking about the Lord Jesus. He went on to speak about the good news of Jesus as they drove along the road.

'Look, over there!' said the Ethiopian. 'Here is some water. Why shouldn't I be baptised? Stop the chariot!' he ordered.

Both men went down to the water and Philip baptised the Ethiopian. He showed that he now believed in the Lord Jesus.

When they came out of the water, Philip was taken away by the Holy Spirit. The Ethiopian did not see him again. He carried on along the road home, rejoicing in the salvation of the Lord. He became a follower of Jesus in a far off land.

Paul

Saul was violently opposed to Jesus and his followers. He had watched as Stephen was stoned to death. He was determined to get rid of as many believers as he could. He travelled to Damascus in the north. His purpose was to arrest followers of Jesus and bring them back to Jerusalem as prisoners.

Saul's life was dramatically changed before he even reached Damascus.

Not far from the town, a bright light from heaven shone on him with a blinding flash. He fell to the ground and heard a voice saying, 'Saul, Saul, why are you persecuting me?'

'Who are you, Lord?' Saul asked.

'I am Jesus, whom you are persecuting,' he replied. 'Go into the city of Damascus and you will be told what to do.'

Saul rose from the ground, but when he opened his eyes, he could see nothing. He had to be led by the hand into Damascus. For three days he was blind. He did not eat or drink anything. He stayed in a house in Straight Street praying.

The Lord spoke in a vision to one of his disciples called Ananias. 'Go to Straight Street, to Judas' house and ask for a man from Tarsus, Saul.'

'Lord, I have heard lots of bad reports about this man,' objected Ananias. 'He has come here to arrest your people.'

'Go,' repeated the Lord. 'This man has been chosen by me to tell both the Gentiles and Jews about me.'

So Ananias went to the house. He placed his hand on Saul and said, 'Brother Saul, the Lord Jesus who appeared to you on the road, has sent me to you, so that you may see again and be filled with the Holy Spirit.'

Immediately Saul could see. He got up and was baptised. He then ate some food — the first for three days — and soon felt strong.

Saul spent several days with the Lord's people in Damascus. He preached in the synagogue that Jesus is the Son of God. The Jews were so perplexed by his words. They planned to kill him. Word of this plot reached Saul and, one dark night, he was helped to escape by being lowered in a basket over the city wall.

This was the start of Saul's life as a follower of Jesus. His name was changed to Paul and he spent many years travelling, preaching God's word whenever he could.

Paul's Fellow Missionaries

Paul had several different helpers and companions on his missionary journeys.

Barnabas, who had been Paul's first friend in Jerusalem after he was converted, went with Paul on his first missionary journey.

They sailed to Cyprus and preached the gospel of Jesus in the synagogues. John Mark, a relative of Barnabas, was with them as a helper. But he left to go back home early.

Paul and Barnabas had many adventures together as they travelled on through present-day Turkey. Many people received their message gladly but several others were angry with them and chased them away.

In Lystra, a crippled man was healed when Paul spoke to him. The crowds were so impressed, they began to worship Paul and Barnabas as gods. This upset the missionaries. 'We are just men like you,' they exclaimed. 'You should worship the living God who made heaven and earth and everything in it.'

The mood of the crowd soon changed when some Jews started speaking against Paul and Barnabas.

The crowd who had been worshipping Paul, now started to stone him. They dragged him outside the town and left him for dead. The believers came to his aid and helped him back to town. He and Barnabas left the next day.

Paul and Barnabas eventually returned to Antioch where they told the local Christians all that God had done through them.

After some time they both wanted to make a return visit to the various church groups. Barnabas wanted to take young John Mark with them again, but Paul objected to this as he had let them down before. So they decided to go their separate ways. Barnabas accompanied by John Mark sailed to Cyprus.

Paul accompanied by Silas set off overland for Turkey and Europe. They were joined on route by a young man, Timothy. His mother and grandmother had taught him the Bible when he was a little boy. He was a great help to Paul and Silas as they preached to the churches throughout Greece. They met many dangers, but as they preached, the word of God powerfully changed people's lives. Many became followers of Jesus.

Lydia

Paul and his friends came to the town of Philippi in the country of Greece. On the Sabbath day, they went out of the town to the riverside where several women were gathered to pray. One of them was Lydia, a well-to-do woman who had a business selling purple cloth. The Lord opened her heart to respond to the gospel message that Paul preached. Quietly she became a follower of Jesus Christ. She and her family were baptised. She showed great hospitality to Paul and his friends, persuading them to stay at her house.

The Philippian Jailer

Paul and his fellow missionary Silas met with opposition from the authorities in Philippi. They accused them of disturbing the peace and had them beaten and thrown in jail. The jailer was ordered to guard them carefully. He put them to an inner cell and fastened their feet securely in the stocks.

Paul and Silas were not down-hearted. At midnight they were praying and singing praise to God, and all in the prison could hear them. Just then there was a violent earthquake. The prison shook, the doors burst open, the chains came loose.

The jailer woke up with a start. In his panic he grabbed his sword and was about to kill himself. His life would not be worth living, he thought, if his important prisoners had escaped. 'Don't harm yourself!' shouted Paul. 'We are all here.'

Trembling, the jailer fell down before Paul and Silas. 'What must I do to be saved?' he asked.

'Believe in the Lord Jesus and you will be saved,' they told him.

Then they preached the word of God to him and to his family and household.

The jailer took them to his house, washed their wounds, and had a fine meal prepared for them. He was baptised to show that he was now a follower of the Lord Jesus.

Priscilla and Aquila

Further on the journey, at Corinth, Paul stayed with a couple, Aquila and his wife Priscilla. By trade they were tentmakers like Paul. So they worked together for a while.

Aquila and Priscilla went with Paul on the next stage of his journey to Ephesus where Paul left them as he carried on to Caesarea.

Aquila and Priscilla served the Lord in Ephesus. They heard a man called Apollos fervently preaching in the synagogue. He had a great knowledge of God's word, but some of his views, especially about baptism, were not right. Priscilla and Aquila asked Apollos to come to their house. They spent some time with him explaining the word of God more fully. As a result Apollos became a much more useful preacher of God's word.

Philemon and Onesimus

Philemon was a prosperous Christian in Colosse. He had a large house with slaves. One of them, Onesimus, ran away after stealing from his master. This was a very grave offence.

Later Onesimus met Paul and heard God's way of salvation from him. Onesimus came to trust in the Lord Jesus as his Saviour too. He became a follower.

Paul then wrote a letter to Onesimus' master, Philemon. Onesimus now wanted to return to his master and ask for forgiveness. Paul asked Philemon to forgive him and accept him as a Christian brother.

THE FOLLOWERS OF JESUS

TODAY'S FOLLOWERS

Those who follow the Lord Jesus have a love
for each other.

ARE YOU A FOLLOWER?
God's message in the Bible is for you. You are
asked to follow the Lord Jesus.

As he said to his disciples, Jesus says to you,
'Follow me.'
First of all you have to repent or tell God that
you are truly sorry for your sins and ask for his
forgiveness. Then you must trust in Jesus
Christ and thank him for his death on the
cross. His word gives you instruction and
makes you wise and happy.